S0-AII-441

BIG NAME HUNTING

"I collect autographic letters for historical reasons."

"I am a collector of original letters written by outstanding figures in American history."

Two famous American collectors

BIG NAME HUNTING

A BEGINNER'S GUIDE TO AUTOGRAPH COLLECTING

BY CHARLES HAMILTON
WITH DIANE HAMILTON

SIMON AND SCHUSTER NEW YORK

Published by Simon and Schuster, Children's Book Division
Rockefeller Center, 630 Fifth Avenue
New York, New York 10020
SBN 65206-0 Reinforced Binding
Library of Congress Catalog Card Number: 72-92158
Manufactured in the United States of America

1 2 3 4 5 6 7 8 9 10

To our daughter

Carolyn Brooks Hamilton

CONTENTS

INTRODUCTION

An autograph letter is the most intimate relic of a great man or woman. Even a signature is interesting, for it may tell us something about the character of the writer; but letters and documents are more significant and valuable, for they are actual fragments of history. Through the letters of distinguished people, living and dead, you can probe into the present and past and discover new facts about your world.

Without letters, documents and manuscripts, there would be no history or literature. Even in ancient Rome there were those who valued autographs. Cicero, the celebrated orator, treasured a letter of Julius Caesar in his collection. (If this letter were to turn up today it would be worth at least a million dollars!) Queen Victoria was an avid collector. In the early nineteenth century, J. P. Morgan used his vast wealth to assemble the world's most important collection. More recently, both Presidents Franklin D. Roosevelt and John F. Kennedy were fascinated by the pursuit of autographs of their fellow Americans, although their collections were not nearly so extensive as Morgan's.

But you don't have to be either wealthy or influential to begin your own collection of autographs. You can often get the autographs of living celebrities for no more than the cost of two postage stamps. Those of famous people no longer living may cost a little more—or they may, as in the case of such scarce and sought-after autographs as Washington's and Lincoln's, be very expensive.

There will be many pitfalls for you as a beginning collector. You will be faced with such things as forgeries, secretarial imitations, photographs so expertly produced that they look almost exactly like their originals, machines that can scrawl an exact duplicate of a person's signature (with his own pen!) and others you'll read about here. But you're sure to find that these traps and decoys will only make your quest more rewarding. For as you read this book you'll discover how to embark on one of the most stimulating of all hobbies. In no other field of collecting can you make such close friends with the people who have changed the course of history and the arts.

1.

HOW TO GET STARTED

A SHEET of paper, a pair of stamped envelopes and a pen. These are all you need to start a fascinating collection of autographs. So let's get started.

Why not begin with a big name—say Billy Graham, the evangelist.

Your letter to Billy Graham should read something like this:

The Reverend William F. Graham
1300 Harmon Place
Minneapolis, Minnesota 55403

Dear Dr. Graham:

I am a boy (or girl)   years old and am forming a collection of autographs of the most famous people of our time. I should be deeply grateful if you would send me your autograph for my collection. For your convenience in replying I am enclosing a stamped, self-addressed envelope.

Thank you in advance.

Respectfully yours,

At least half of the people to whom you write will send you a signature. Longfellow once mailed out seventy of his autographs in a single day. "I always like to do this little favor," he said. "It is so little to do, to write your name on a card; and if I didn't do it some boy or girl might be looking, day by day, for the postman and be disappointed."

You may decide that you would like to have autographs all on cards of identical size. If so, just enclose a card or blank page from your autograph album with each request for a signature.

The list of unusual collections you might form is as endless as your own ingenuity. Here are some examples to fuel your imagination:

Signed sketches or caricatures. If you have artistic talent, you might make a celebrity sketch yourself. You could form a fascinating gallery of signed portraits, sending each to your subject for his signature. A friend, Jack Rosen, is a skilled caricaturist. He has built a very valuable collection of original signed drawings, including many presidents. Jack sometimes makes two caricatures and invites his correspondent to keep one for himself and to sign and return the other.

Signed photographs. While it is a good idea to furnish your own photographs, many noted people, especially actors and actresses, will send you a signed photograph if you ask for one. I find signed photographs far more interesting than mere signatures.

Signed checks. Some years ago an enterprising collector devised a plan for "swapping" checks with noted men and women. He sent each his own check for one cent and asked if each would send his own

Caricature of Bob Hope by Jack Rosen, signed by the noted comedian.

Guaranty Trust Company of New York 1-107
Fifth Avenue Office
No 1000 New York May 30th 1925
Pay to the order of Waldo C. Moore
One Cent Dollars
Payable through the New York Clearing House
$ 01/100 Franklin D Roosevelt

Check for one cent signed by Franklin D. Roosevelt

check for a penny in exchange. The personal check sent to him by Franklin D. Roosevelt is today worth fifty thousand times its face value!

Signed art reproductions. You can easily get beautiful color reproductions of the important paintings of contemporary artists in posters, books, postcards and —less expensively—in magazines. A fine reproduction is, of course, more valuable when signed than a folded and wrinkled one, so be sure to pack and ship your treasures with care.

Signature of Frank Lloyd Wright

The late Frank Lloyd Wright, perhaps the greatest architect of modern times, was always delighted to sign photographs of his buildings for collectors. Today these are worth fifty dollars or more.

Among those painters who have been very generous to collectors, in response to a sincere appeal, are Salvador Dali, Picasso and Andrew Wyeth.

Signatures of Dali and Picasso

There are other special ways to form a collection, including some that are pretty offbeat. I know several ladies who are gathering autographs signed on squares of white cotton with the idea of embroidering over each signature and making a "celebrity quilt."

2.

WHAT TO COLLECT

Collect the autographs that interest you. There are so many varied fields that your choice is almost unlimited. But your collection will be far more intriguing if you stick to two or three or, at most, five areas, rather than assembling unrelated odds and ends.

Some of the most popular fields are:

SPORTS HEROES
MOVIE STARS
STATESMEN
AUTHORS
COMPOSERS AND MUSICIANS
ASTRONAUTS
PRESIDENTS
ARTISTS

Should you decide to collect the autographs of the heroes of the sporting pages, you will find that your collection will naturally divide itself into many categories, such as football, baseball, boxing and golf. Few

Modern Judaica is a popular field of interest. Above is the signature of Israeli military hero, Moshe Dayan.

Black leaders of America. A new field of collecting is in the field of Negro culture. Above are signatures of Frederick Douglass, noted one-time slave and lecturer, and Martin Luther King, Jr., famed civil rights leader.

Signatures of Hemingway and Faulkner

sports figures have enjoyed the permanent fame of Babe Ruth, Jim Thorpe or John L. Sullivan, so that a great many of the names in your collection will be forgotten in the course of a few years.

On the other hand, if you collect in the most popular of all fields—presidents—you will have to venture into the past and buy from dealers or possibly trade with other collectors for the autographs of the presidents who are no longer living.

If you are a movie buff, by all means collect signed photographs of movie stars! But in this field, as in that of sports, reputations fade quickly and the stars of today are often the forgotten people of tomorrow. I recently examined a collection of nearly two hundred signed photographs of movie celebrities dating back to the early 1920's, and I found less than a dozen whose names or faces I could recognize.

Of far more permanent interest and value are the autographs of authors and composers. The fortunate collector of a few years ago who received a letter from Ernest Hemingway or William Faulkner now finds that it is worth several hundred dollars.

An extremely popular field with young collectors is the astronauts. The first great American astronaut, John Glenn, has always been generous with his signature and it is present in nearly every collection. Much more difficult to get are the autographs of the Russian astronauts, since many of them don't reply to requests for their signatures. One of the rarest is Titov. During his visit to the United States a few years ago, Titov finished a pack of Russian cigarettes and tossed away the empty wrapper. An alert young collector pounced on it and asked the Russian astronaut to sign it for him. Titov smilingly obliged.

Whatever fields of collecting you adventure into, you will find that your interest and enthusiasm grow with every new acquisition!

Commemorative first-day cover signed by Scott Carpenter.

3.

HOW TO BUILD AN IMPORTANT COLLECTION

A YOUNG MAN asked me not long ago: "Is it really possible to get together a valuable autograph collection only for the cost of stationery and postage?"

"Certainly," I told him, "but you will need just a little more."

"What's that?" he wanted to know.

"You'll need imagination," I said. "And ingenuity and an instinct for what is exciting. These make the difference between a dull and a fascinating collection. And the only really valuable collections are those that are full of unusual and imaginative autographs.

"Let's take the example of Hitler's successor, Grand Admiral Karl Dönitz, the last of the Nazi rulers. His signature," I explained, "has only a small value, for it is nothing more than evidence that Dönitz knows how to write his name. But when it's signed to an important document—say his order to ratify the surrender of the German army to the Allies—it becomes an important historic relic."

"Do you think I could possibly get such a document signed for my own collection?" the young man asked eagerly.

I assured him that he could. "Others have done it, and you can, too!

Dönitz
6. Nov. 1968

INSTRUMENT OF SURRENDER OF ALL GERMAN FORCES
TO GENERAL DWIGHT D. EISENHOWER,
SUPREME COMMANDER OF THE ALLIED EXPEDITIONARY FORCES,
AND TO THE SOVIET HIGH COMMAND

Rheims, May 7, 1945.

1. We the undersigned, acting by authority of the German High Command, hereby surrender unconditionally to the Supreme Commander, Allied Expeditionary Force and simultaneously to the Soviet High Command all forces on land, sea, and in the air who are at this date under German control.

2. The German High Command will at once issue orders to all German military, naval and air authorities and to all forces under German control to cease active operations at 2301 hours Central European time on 8 May and to remain in the positions occupied at that time. No ship, vessel, or aircraft is to be scuttled, or any damage done to their hull, machinery or equipment.

3. The German High Command will at once issue to the appropriate commanders, and ensure the carrying out of any further orders issued by the Supreme Commander, Allied Expeditionary Force and by the Soviet High Command.

4. This act of military surrender is without prejudice to, and will be superseded by any general instrument of surrender imposed by, or on behalf of the United Nations and applicable to Germany and the German armed forces as a whole.

5. In the event of the German High Command or any of the forces under their control failing to act in accordance with this Act of Surrender, the Supreme Commander, Allied Expeditionary Force and the Soviet High Command will take such punitive or other action as they deem appropriate.

Signed at Rheims at 0241 on the 7th day of May, 1945.

Souvenir copy of Grand Admiral Dönitz' order to surrender the Nazi army, signed for a collector

"First you must get the German text of Dönitz' surrender order and then type or hand-letter it carefully. Mail it to him with a courteous request that he sign it for you."

My young friend did write to the old admiral, and he was thrilled when he got a signed copy of one of the most famous documents in the history of this century!

This is just one example of how a beginning collector used his ingenuity instead of his pocketbook to make a valuable addition to his autograph collection. I'm sure you'll have lots of unusual ideas of your own for adding unique documents to your collection. Your imagination and interests must guide you.

Why not try to get your favorite poets to write out a stanza or two from their best-known poems? The late Carl Sandburg was most friendly

Signature of Carl Sandburg

toward youthful autograph seekers and occasionally signed typescripts of his brief but beautiful "Fog." Such literary treasures readily sell today for $50 to $75!

Or why not write a polite letter to a novelist you admire, enclosing a one-page excerpt from his most celebrated book, and ask him to put his signature on it. Most authors are very busy, but nearly all will be glad to do this favor for a boy or girl.

Although John Steinbeck was a notorious recluse he, too, was always glad to oblige young collectors. Often I come across signed typescripts from his famous novels. Naturally they are very valuable today.

When you write for an autograph, always make your request a sincere one. If you admire an author or statesman, tell him so. If you do not, but want his autograph anyway, simply make an honest and direct request.

The more you use your imagination, the more amazing and valuable your collection will become. Fill it with intriguing and controversial signed comments by authors, artists, statesmen, composers and military leaders. Watch the newspapers carefully and, whenever you run across an unusual or important comment by any public figure, copy it out longhand or on a typewriter and send it to him with a request that he sign it. If the newspaper doesn't give you a clue to his address, try *Who's Who in America,* the *International Who's Who,* or *Celebrity Register,* volumes you'll find in your local library. If you are alert to the latest developments in history and literature, music and art, you'll soon accumulate an extremely significant and valuable collection.

One of America's leading young autograph dealers, Bruce Gimelson of Philadelphia, got his start as a wide-awake boy of seven.

"I was sitting in the back seat of our car as we traveled along Philadelphia's West River Drive. When we pulled up for a stop light, to my great excitement, in the limousine next to us was the late Connie Mack, for fifty years the owner and manager of the Philadelphia Athletics baseball team. I rolled down the window and yelled, 'Hi, Connie! Can I have your autograph?'

"In a twinkle he handed me a signed card . . . and this started me on my way."

Another alert young collector told me that, as a boy, he had met the famous American poet, Edna St. Vincent Millay.

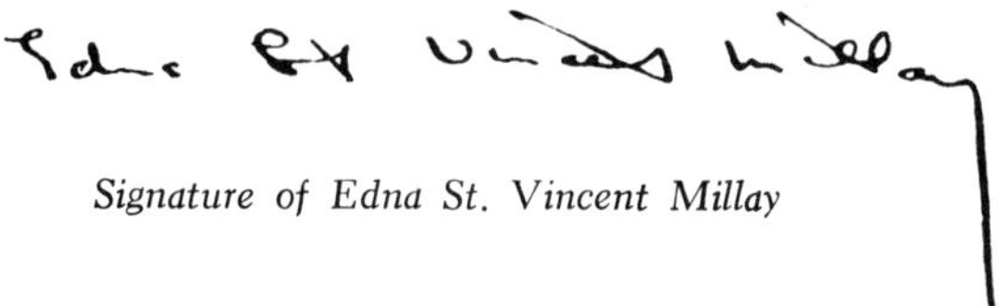

Signature of Edna St. Vincent Millay

"I was in a theater," the collector explained, "and during the intermission I suddenly heard a buzz of excitement. Someone pointed out to me a pretty, distinguished-looking woman. 'That's Miss Millay,' he told me.

"Quickly I whipped out my fountain pen and on a scrap of paper wrote out from memory her famous quatrain beginning, 'I burn my candle at both ends.' I then placed it before her and asked her to sign it.

"Although she had a reputation for refusing her autograph to collectors, she seemed amused and I think impressed by my alertness and readily signed her famous poem."

When I paid the man $60 for this document, I smiled and said, "This is what you get for being a quick-thinking boy!"

4.

HOW TO BUY FROM DEALERS

NOT LONG AGO I was chatting with a young collector who told me proudly: "Not a single autograph in my collection was bought from a dealer. Every one of them was a gift from the writer!"

I congratulated him, for he had a very interesting and, in many ways, significant collection. On the other hand, it contained only the autographs of living people.

"Don't you think your collection would be even more fascinating—and certainly more complete—if you were to strengthen your presidential series?"

"Naturally," the young man agreed, "I'd like to add some autographs of presidents who are no longer living. I have a few autographs I'd be willing to swap with other collectors, but I'm not quite sure how to go about that. And I'm a little afraid to buy from dealers because I don't know anything about values. I would have no way of telling whether I was paying the right price or way too much for an autograph if I bought it from a catalogue."

"Once in a while it's possible to add an important autograph to your collection by swapping," I said. And in the Appendix to this book are listed the American autograph societies. Any collector can write to them asking for the names of their members. Some of these members may be willing to trade.

"But," I went on, "there's no reason to be afraid of buying from dealers. You needn't worry about getting your money's worth, because most well-known dealers are entirely reliable. Occasionally a dealer may accidently overcharge or even undercharge for an autograph, but in general their prices are quite similar to one another and quite fair. If one dealer were consistently to charge much more for comparable autographs than all the other dealers, he simply couldn't remain in business. And, once in a while, you may pick up a real bargain.

"In the terms of sale listed at the front of every reliable dealer's catalogue, you will find an unconditional guarantee of authenticity. Should any autograph you buy prove to be a forgery, a facsimile or a copy, your money will be refunded immediately."

I then explained the abbreviations used by dealers. As you perhaps know, the term *autograph* doesn't necessarily refer to a signature but may describe *any* handwritten letter, document or manuscript. Here are the common abbreviations and their meanings:

A.L.S.—Autograph (handwritten) Letter Signed
L.S.—Letter Signed (typed or written by a secretary)

$3.50 Per Item
No Approvals, No Returns

HALL, G. Stanley, Amer. psychologist, educator, Sig.; HALL, Marie, Eng. violinist, p.c. photo, Sgd.; HAMLIN, Hannibal, V.P.U.S., Sig.; HANCOCK, W.S., Union Gen., Sig.; HAPGOOD, Norman, Amer. ed., writer, ALS; HARDELOT, Guy d', Fr. composer of songs sung by Calvé, Melba, etc., ALS; HARE, Sir John, Eng. actor, Sig. on card & p.c. photo, mounted; HARLAN, James, Sec. Int., ADS; HARLAN, J., LS; HARLAN, John M., Just. U.S. Sup. Ct., ANS; HARPER, Wm. R., Amer. educator, 1st Pres. Univ. of Chicago, LS; *HARPER'S WEEKLY*, complete issue, July 24, 1869; HARPIGNIES, Henri, Fr. landscape painter, ALS; HARRIS, Joel Chandler, Amer. writer, creator Uncle Remus tales, Sig. & date; HARRIS, Laurence W., cartoonist, illustrator, ALS; HART, Albert B., historian, educator, LS; HARTLEY, J. Scott, Amer. sculptor, ALS, trimmed; HARVEY, Geo. B., journalist, ed., dipl., ALS; HARVEY, Martin, Eng. actor, manager, Sig. on card & p.c. photo, mounted; HATHORN, John, M.O.C., Speaker, N.Y.Assembly, DS; HAW-TREY, Sir Charles, Eng. actor, manager. Sig. on card & trimmed p.c. photo, mounted; HAY, Stuart, cartoonist, illustrator, ALS; HAYES, Isaac I., arctic explorer, surgeon, Sig.; HAYS, Arthur G., civil liberties lawyer, LS; HAYS, Harry T., Maj. Gen. CSA, Sig. & rank.

HEINTZELMAN, Sam. P., Union Gen., Sig.; HENDERSON, Tom, cartoonist, ALS; HENDRICKS, Thos. A., V.P.U.S., Sig.; HENRY, Joseph, 1st Dir. Smithsonian Inst., scientist, Sig. & date; HERRMANN, Alex., magician, Sig.; HERRON, Francis J., Union Gen., Medal of Honor, Sig. on check; HERTZ, Alfred, Germ. Met. Op. conductor, LS; HILL, B.H., Sen. CSA & U.S., Sig.; HITCHCOCK, E.A., Maj. Gen. U.S. Vols., grandson of Ethan Allen, Sig., HOKE, Robt. F., Maj. Gen. CSA, Sig. & rank, pencil; HOLT, Joseph, P.M.Gen., Sec. War, Prosecutor Lincoln assass. conspirators, Sig.; HOOKER, Isabella B., advocate women's rights, philanthropist, ALS; [HOOVER, Herbert], engraved card acknowledging expression of sympathy upon death of Mrs. Hoover; HOOVER, J. Edgar, Dir. FBI, LS; HORNADAY, Wm.T., zoologist, promoter of wildlife protection, ALS; HOW-ARD, Bronson, Amer. dramatist, Sig. & p.c. photo, mounted; HOWE, Julia Ward, Amer. suffragist, composer *Battle Hymn of the Republic*, Sig. & date; HOWELLS, Wm. Dean, writer, ed., critic, Sig.; HUGHES, John J., R.C. Archbshp. N.Y., laid cornerstone St. Patrick's, Sig.; HUGHES, Rupert, Amer. author, ALS, corres. card; HUGHES, R., LS; HUME, Fergus, Eng. writer detective stories, AQS; HUME, Joseph, Eng. radical politician, "Adversity Hume", Sig.; HUMPHREYS, Andrew A, Union Gen., Sig. & rank; [HUNGARIAN FUND], $1 note bearing L. Kossuth's Sig. in reproduction; HUNTER, David, Union Gen., Pres. Mil. Commission that tried Lincoln assass. conspirators, Sig. & rank; HUTCHESON, Ernest, pianist, composer, Pres. Juilliard, Sig., inscrip. & date.

ILLINGTON, Margaret, Amer. actress, m. Daniel Frohman, ALS; [INDENTURE], for 73-1/2 acres of land in N.J., torn; [INDENTURE], for lease of school lot owned by Selectman of Huntington, Vt.; INGALLS, John J., orator, U.S. Sen., Kans., ALS: INGE, Wm. R., Eng. scholar, writer, Dean St. Paul, ANS; INGELOW, Jean, Eng. poet, novelist, ALS: INGERSOLL, Chas. J., Pa. Memb. Cong., ALS; INGERSOLL, Ernest, Amer. naturalist, ALS; INGERSOLL, Robt. G., noted agnostic lecturer, ALS; INGERSOLL, R.G., Sig.; INGHAM, Sam. D., Sec. Treas., 2 lines & Sig. as Sec. Treas.; INNITZER, Theodore, Cardinal Archbshp. of Vienna, Anti-Nazi W.W. II, Sig.; IRVING, Henry, Famous Eng. actor, Sig.; IRVING, Jay, cartoonist, creator of N.Y.P.D.'s "Willie Doodle", LS; IRWIN, May, famous comic actress, ALS; IRWIN, Wallace, Amer. journalist, humorist, LS; IRWIN, Will, Amer. journalist, writer, LS to Grace H. Conkling, poet; IS-TRATI, Panait, Rumanian novelist, AQS; JACKSON, Howell E., CSA Gen., Sig.; JACK-SON, Robert H., Just. U.S. Sup. Ct., chief prosecutor, Nuremburg, Sig. on Sup. Ct. card; JACOBI, Abraham, noted pediatrician, ADS; JAKOBOWSKI, E. operetta composer, ANS; JAMES, Henry, Amer. lawyer, biographer, Sig. & 5 others on card; JANAUSCHEK, Fanny, Bohemian tragedienne, toured U.S., AQS; JANAUSCHEK, ANS; JARVIS, Thos. J., Gov. N.C., CSA officer, ALS; JASTROW, Morris, Semitic scholar, ALS; JEWETT, Sarah Orne, Amer. author, Sig.; JOFFRE, J.H.C., "Papa", C. in C. Fr. Army, hero Battle of Marne W.W. I, Sig. & date; JOHANSEN, John C., Danish-Amer. portrait painter, ALS; JOHNSON, Bradley T., Brig. Gen. CSA, Sig.; JOHNSON, Reverdy, defended Dred Scott,

Page from a catalogue issued by Walter R. Benjamin Autographs, Inc., of New York. Every item is priced at only $3.50.

A.D.S.—Autograph Document Signed
D.S.—Document Signed
A.Ms.S.—Autograph Manuscript Signed
A.Q.S.—Autograph Quotation Signed
4to—A page about 8″ x 10″
8vo—A page about 5″ x 7″
16mo—A very small sheet

Generally speaking, the most sought-after form of autograph is the A.L.S., which is entirely in the hand of the writer and signed by him—as opposed to the L.S., a letter in the handwriting of a secretary or else typewritten and merely signed by the writer.

Once you begin buying from dealers you will find it great sport, since you'll be able to start improving your collection very quickly at small cost. For as little as five or ten dollars a month you might collect, in the course of a year, a dozen or more signatures such as those of Daniel Webster, P. T. Barnum, and Henry W. Longfellow.

Signature of Daniel Webster

Signature of Henry W. Longfellow

Full letters of such famous men, of course, are much more expensive. You will soon discover that a fine or interesting A.L.S. commands a price many times that of a signature. Less costly—but only slightly less—are letters that were dictated and merely signed by the writer. The cost of a document signed by a famous person, unless its content is unusual or remarkable, is generally less than that of letters.

So that you can write to the leading dealers in the country for their catalogues, there is a list of reliable autograph dealers in the Appendix. Many dealers charge a small sum for catalogues, especially when they are very costly to print, but most dealers will

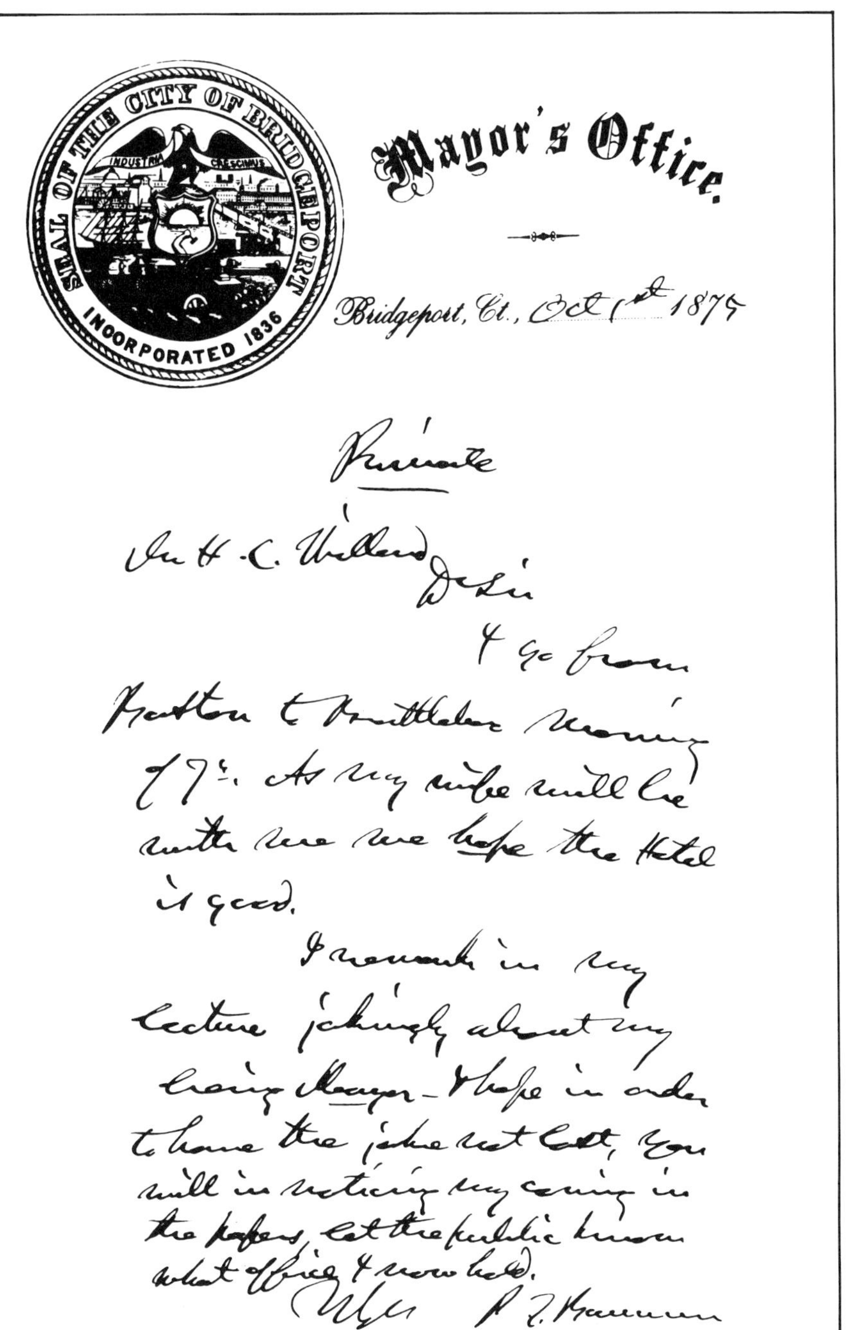

SEAL OF THE CITY OF BRIDGEPORT
INDUSTRIA CRESCIMUS
INCORPORATED 1836

Mayor's Office.

Bridgeport, Ct., Oct 1st 1875

Private

Dr H. C. Willard
Dr Sir

I go from Boston to Brattleboro morning of 7th. As my wife will be with me we hope the Hotel is good.

I remark in my lecture jokingly about my being Mayor — I hope in order to have the joke not lost, you will in noticing my coming in the papers, let the public know what office I now hold.

Yrs P. T. Barnum

Handwritten letter (A.L.S.) of P. T. Barnum

send the first catalogue free. You may not receive additional catalogues unless you make a purchase or buy a year's subscription to the catalogue.

It is a good idea to buy from a number of dealers before settling upon a favorite. David Battan, now a California dealer, recalled to me: "Soon after I placed my name on dealers' lists, I found that the dealers were most eager to help me collect. I learned a lot about autographs through dealers' catalogues—prices, what is collected, what is available, and why people collect autographs. I would suggest to the young collector that he get on as many dealers' mailing lists as possible. He will find that most reliable dealers are eager to assist and guide him."

Once you find the one or more dealers who suit you best, you can let them know exactly what you are looking for and they will be glad to help you build up your collection and fill the gaps in it.

Signature of the Duke of Wellington, Prime Minister of England and victor over Napoleon at Waterloo. His signature may be obtained from dealers for only a few dollars.

The noted Bridgewater, Massachusetts, dealer, Paul C. Richards, advises: "I would recommend that a new collector visit one of the established dealers at his earliest opportunity. He can then seek out the counsel of the dealer, and discuss the area or areas in which he wishes to collect. The dealer will inform him of the availability of material (that is, the amount of said material coming on the market) and the price range of this material. With this information the collector will know what his chances are to form the collection he has in mind and its approximate cost.

"My advice to a person with moderate capital is to specialize in collecting a person or group of persons that has been heretofore neglected by librarians and collectors. This type of material is quite modest in price and yet can convey the excitement and pleasure of collecting. For example, Edward Everett, the famous orator and friend of Lincoln, whom I collected in the mid-1950's, is still not seriously collected today. The vice-presidents and cabinet officers are good groups to collect. Prime ministers of England have been another sadly neglected field. Certain composers and performers can also be obtained at low cost."

Buying from dealers quickly becomes a sport as well as an investment and, aside from the pleasure and knowledge you will gain from your purchases, they may eventually be worth much more than you paid for them. Recently I sold at auction for $350 an ornate ship's papers signed by both Jefferson and Madison. I did not notice until after I sold it that in a corner was penciled a dealer's price of about ten years earlier—fifteen dollars!

Signatures of Thomas Jefferson and James Madison

5.

AUCTIONS ARE FUN

Alec Chanin is an enthusiastic young collector. He and his father are avid autograph buyers, who purchase mostly at auction. The last time I saw Alec he was fresh from a summer spent pitching hay on a farm, and he had an eager, intent look about him. I asked him how he felt about bidding at auction.

"I love the excitement of it," he told me. "My father and I go over the material before the sale and decide what autographs we want to buy and how much we can bid. Then I do the bidding."

"What has been your biggest auction thrill so far, Alec?" I asked him.

"Well," he told me, "I'm a Civil War buff. I like to read about soldiers—and I like their letters to friends at home. So my greatest thrill came when I beat out a large institution in Ohio for a collection of letters written by an Ohio soldier during the Civil War."

"How did you know the underbidder was an Ohio institution?"

"That's part of the fascination of bidding—to find out who's bidding against you. I always watch the rest of the room while I bid."

Alec Chanin's understanding of the importance of *letters* with *content*, as opposed to mere *signatures*, pleased me greatly. I asked him to

there are within about 58-
rods of us two 32 pounder
~~Parrott~~ Parrott guns that
are throwing Shells every
few minutes and once in
a while it makes me
jump a little for it comes
so suddenly But I think
I will close for this time
As it is very warm and
I have one more Letter
to write today Hoping to
address you next from
Richmond I remain as
Ever your own Son
& Brother

Remember me to all
who inquire and accept
much Love for yourselves
Again Yours &c

Chas. C. Kinsman

Last page of a Civil War soldier's letter describing a bombardment explain to me what he felt was so dramatic about the letters of common soldiers. I was just as pleased with his reply:

"Letters of the ordinary soldier intrigue me because they show his attitude toward killing—his ideas about battle. History is much more interesting when you follow the common soldier. And the Confederate soldier is especially exciting, because he had less of everything."

Young Chanin may some day become a famous collector because he has already discovered what it takes to form an exciting collection and he has learned to exploit the joys of bidding at auction.

In recent years, more and more successful auction bidders are youngsters or beginning collectors. They are discovering that one of the most fascinating ways to buy or sell autographs is at a public sale. In the course of a year, millions of dollars worth of letters and documents change hands at auction. But don't let those figures scare you! Sometimes an entire collection of fifty to one hundred autographs is "knocked down" or sold to some lucky bidder for only fifteen or twenty dollars.

Here's how an auction works. Before every scheduled sale, the auction house prepares a catalogue in which each lot (numbered item or items) is carefully described. Occasionally such catalogues are offered without charge, but generally the auction house will ask you to pay for at least a part of the cost of preparing and printing the catalogue, perhaps one or two dollars. You will find in the Appendix to this book the names and addresses of the leading auction houses that handle autographs.

In many catalogues, you will discover printed after each lot an estimate of what it may be expected to fetch. The actual price you pay may at times be only a fraction of the estimate. Or you may have to pay many times the estimate since, at best, the estimate is only an educated guess by the auctioneer.

After you receive your catalogue, read it carefully and decide which lots you wish to bid on. If you can attend the sale in person, you'll find it a very exciting experience. It takes no special skill to bid. You simply raise your hand when you want to increase the amount of the current bid. The auctioneer will let you know if you accidentally bid against

Public Auction Sale Number Fifty-Six

CHARLES HAMILTON GALLERIES, INC.
25 East 77th Street
New York, N.Y. 10021

Please buy for me at your sale on Mar. 9, 1972 the lots below. The amounts listed are my limit on each lot and I understand that you will purchase for me as much below this price as possible. I have read the terms of sale carefully and agree to abide by them.

References: PREVIOUS BIDDER

Very truly yours,
WILLIAM THOMAS
1011 WEST DRIVE
NEW YORK, N.Y. 1002

Lot	Bid		Lot	Bid		Lot	Bid	
16	15	00						
108	25	00						
117	10	00						
230	20	00						
309	30	00						

LIST OF PRICES REALIZED—$1.00

Bid sheet for an auction at Charles Hamilton Galleries, Inc.

yourself by saying something like, "The bid I have is that of the young man in the third row on my right." At most auctions, the auctioneer has one or two spotters. A spotter is a man or woman who helps him to catch all the bids.

The easiest way to bid at auction, though not necessarily the most exciting, is by mail. You study the estimate, if there is one printed in the catalogue, and decide how much you want to pay. Then, on the bid sheet form provided in every catalogue, you fill in the number and the highest amount you are willing to bid, then mail the sheet to the auction house. On receipt, your bid sheet is numbered (in case of tie bids the lot is sold to the person whose bid sheet was received first) and your bid or bids will be entered in an order book and used competitively against floor bidders during the sale. You may be lucky and buy a lot for only a fraction of your bid. Such things happen at every sale!

More and more, I find that youthful collectors, as well as the more experienced ones, are turning to auctions as a pleasant and inexpensive means of building up their collections. One fifteen-year-old boy who used to attend my sales (before his family moved West) bought at bargain prices many letters of Franklin D. Roosevelt, whom he especially admired.

Sooner or later, you will probably turn to auction bidding to enhance your collection with unusual or important autographs. Like many others, you will discover that it is a truly great adventure.

6.

HOW TO PRESERVE AND DISPLAY YOUR COLLECTION

The other day I was leafing through an autograph collection someone had sent me for an offer. Most of the letters were very neat looking and well-preserved, but I saw nothing that looked exciting. It didn't appear as if the collection contained anything of value.

"Everything here is in such fine condition," I said to my secretary. "I wonder why that's always the case. The worthless collections are almost always perfectly preserved!"

Then suddenly I noticed between the other letters a faded, ragged document, pasted on a second sheet of paper. "Wait a minute!" I shouted. "Here's something that's bound to be valuable! See the terrible condition it's in, and how it's been mounted. It's got to be good. I'll bet, before I even look at it, that the signature is right over the fold so that it's partially worn off; and there are sure to be several words completely eaten away by Scotch-tape stains."

A few months earlier, when my secretary had just begun to work for me, she would have thought I was joking. But now she just smiled wryly: "I wish I didn't know you're probably right, Mr. Hamilton!"

Sure enough, when I fished the letter out of the pile, it was a once-beautiful letter of John F. Kennedy, written to a young autograph collector. "See, here it is. It was the only really valuable letter in this boy's collection, but now it's worth about fifteen dollars instead of the hundred dollars I could have offered if the owner hadn't tampered with it. See, all the congressmen and senators and these obscure state officials—all of them in mint condition! That's because he left them alone. But not this one!

"Look, he tested the signature with a drop of water to see if it was genuine and would smudge. It was and it did. And he's even got the letter mounted on cardboard with glue, so that it can't be removed. I wish he'd mounted all the other letters in his collection and left this one alone."

Hitler himself, with all his book-burning, can hardly have done half the harm to recorded history as all the rolls of Scotch tape and glue pots in the hands of overzealous collectors. If I were to produce a brochure listing all the *don'ts* for beginning collectors, at the top of the list would be these words: *Never touch any autograph with Scotch tape or rubber cement!*

Here are a few additional and very important "don'ts" for you to remember:

Don't use glue or mucilage to mount autographs in an album. Both leave ugly, unremovable stains.

Don't trim or cut away the margins of letters or documents or photographs.

Don't retrace penciled or faded autographs. A retraced signature is very little better than no signature at all and its value is almost completely destroyed by retracing.

Don't cut signatures from letters or documents. They are far more interesting and desirable—and valuable—when they're left untouched, just as originally written.

Don't staple your autographs, and avoid paper clips if possible. If your autographs are already stapled or paper-clipped together, try to remove the staples or clips very carefully. Otherwise they will rust and leave ugly stains.

Don't store your autographs in a very damp or very warm place. In a damp spot, autographs are likely to mildew; in a warm, dry place, such as above a radiator or heater, they may become dry and brittle and crumble at a touch.

Don't hang framed autographs where the sun will shine directly on them, even for a short period of the day. Most ink fades when exposed to direct sunlight.

Now that I've told you most of the *don'ts,* let me give you some tips on ways you *can* care for your collection cheaply, easily and safely.

The best way to preserve your autographs is simply to place them between cellulose acetate leaves (for sale at any stationery store) or in individual manila folders, each carefully labeled with its contents for quick reference. The chief advantage to either of these two methods is that you may remove your autographs without difficulty for framing or display or shifting to another category in your collection. Further, the autographs will be left in their original states without mutilation of any kind.

If you wish to mount your autographs in an album, be sure to use an album with fine quality paper. Cheap paper gives off a gas that may stain or brown or even crumble into dust the autographs mounted on it. As an adhesive, use only ordinary, inexpensive, white library paste, which you can buy in any ten-cent store. It won't stain or damage your autographs in any way. Apply only a very little bit at the top corners of your letter, leaving the two bottom corners loose. If you apply too much paste, the paper may wrinkle or warp.

It is best never to attempt repairs without professional help. But if you should decide to try repairing your own autographs, remember our most important *don't.* Don't *ever* use any Scotch tape or rubber cement. Use only tiny strips of tissue paper and lightly paste them with white library paste over the tear or hole you wish to repair. In extreme cases, when a letter is badly worn at all the folds and the paper is very heavy, it is best to find another sheet of paper as close as possible in weight and color to your own document. Cut this into narrow strips about one-half inch wide and then paste them lightly on the reverse side of your letter at the folds. You may want to place the autograph, while the paste is still damp, between two plain pieces of paper or between the pages of an old, worthless book and pile a few heavy books on top of that so that the letter will dry flat and wrinkle-free.

You should arrange your collection according to your own taste. It's a good idea to keep each category in a separate folder or series of folders, with labels such as: American Authors, English Authors, Actors, Artists, Statesmen. This will make it easy for you to put your hands on any autographs at a moment's notice, and it will also help you to get the most possible use and pleasure from your collection.

7.

ROBOTS THAT WRITE SIGNATURES

ONLY A FEW days ago I had a telephone call from a man named Harvey Huston to tell me about a revolutionary new handwriting machine. As president of the Signa-Signer company, Mr. Huston explained that his device has completely outmoded the famous Autopen 50, which signs anybody's signature and can sign three thousand in a single working day.

Mr. Huston went on to say that his machine, for which a patent has just been issued, can add signatures and handwritten postscripts to letters, or even write entire letters. I asked him to tell me how this remarkable machine operates.

"Very simply," he said. "All you do is plug a special message-recording pen into the Signa-Signer (left or right side, depending upon which hand you write with) and then write your message. It is electronically put on a magnetic tape cartridge. Then, when fed

Sincerely,

Harvey Huston

Harvey L. Huston
President

P. S. I look forward to hearing from you soon,

Signature and postscript written with the Signa-Signer

either manually or automatically, the Signa-Signer will write your message an infinite number of times."

I asked whether the message could be identified as machine-written by its pattern.

"The work of the Signa-Signer will be very hard to detect," he answered. "The reason is that the writer can pen a dozen or more identical messages on the same magnetic tape cartridge, each of which will differ slightly from the others, then use them in rotation. So the chance of getting two identical messages and signatures for comparison is only one in twelve. Thus, the writing will pass as an original handwritten message."

Quite different in its method of operation is the Autopen 50, a robot which does its job very simply. To a specially built rotating cylinder, not unlike a huge phonograph record, is affixed a device shaped like a boomerang on which are curves and indentations that, when rotating through two metal posts,

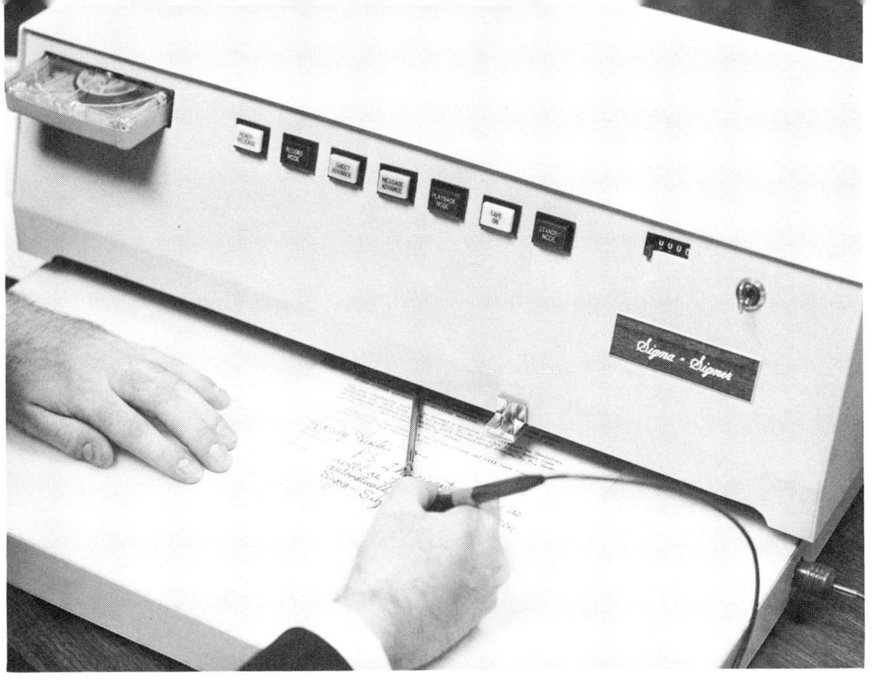

Recording an original signature and message on the Signa-Signer

Playback of handwriting. The original message is instantly ready to be played back thousands of times. Among other uses, the Signa-Signer company suggests that publishers could use their machine "to provide copies of autographed books from their authors."

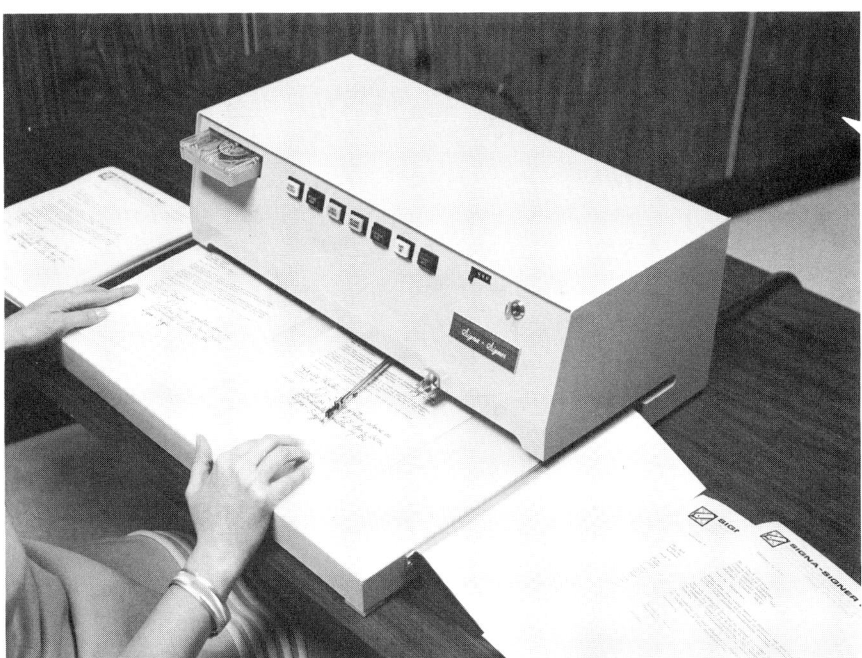

cause your own pen, secured to a steel grip, to write your name perfectly with incredible speed.

How can you spot a robot signature? It's very easy! Simply by holding two of them up to the light, so that they will superimpose. No one ever signs his name exactly the same way twice, but the Autopen, ignoring this fact, writes every name with the identical pattern originally provided by the person who wishes his signature mass produced. If you have no other example for comparison, or if the signature is on a photograph, it is best to consult an expert.

Very few persons will admit that they use the robot. The President denies it. Vice-President Agnew admitted to its use, promised to reform, but only a few days later was back to the machine. In a letter to collector Fred Casoni of Newark, New Jersey, Hubert H. Humphrey wrote: "Yes, we have an autopen which signs my name on mail that I have authorized to be so signed. Some weeks there are thousands of letters going out of this office in response to constituents and others writing about legislative issues before the Congress. Many of these include replies to petitions and mail prompted by organizations and special-interest groups urging letters to members of Congress. I think my time is best spent working on these legislative matters rather than sitting at my desk for many hours a day just signing letters. I am sure the correspondent is well aware that he is one of many expressing themselves on an issue or wanting to know my position and is satisfied with the response. This has been a standard practice for years in almost all Congressional offices."

According to the National Space Agency, all of the

astronauts personally sign autographs when requested, but Alan Shepard, Jr., the famous moon explorer and chief of the Astronaut Office, admitted: "We make every effort to provide actual autographs. This is not, however, always compatible with the demands of our official schedules and, in the case of bulk distribution, it is sometimes necessary to use facsimile signatures." Of the dozens of astronaut autographs which have come my way, most of them on ornate stamped envelopes or photographs, very few were authentic. In my opinion it is doubtful the astronauts sign anything except for personal friends or when cornered at a party or reception. The same is true of the Russian astronauts, whose time is far too precious for them to invest in signing their names for collectors.

Even more confusing and deceptive are the Autopen signatures of the recent presidents—John F. Kennedy, Lyndon B. Johnson and Richard Nixon. Many signed photographs and cards are sent out from the White House with "authentications" written and signed by one of the President's secretaries. They read something like this: "I spoke to the President about your request and he was delighted to sign the enclosed photograph for you. He wants you to know that he greatly appreciates your expressions of esteem." The "signed" photographs which accompany these spurious authentications are, of course, worthless.

Not long ago a young man came into my shop with a "signed" photograph of President Kennedy.

"I am sorry to say," I told him, "that this photo was not actually signed by the President. It has an Autopen signature and is valueless."

Three different Autopen signatures of Neil Armstrong (Courtesy of Paul J. Carr and The Pen and Quill*)*

Robot signatures of John F. Kennedy, Lyndon B. Johnson and Richard M. Nixon. Written in pen and ink by the Autopen 50.

He gave me a smug smile. "Impossible! I was with the President when he signed it."

The young man continued to insist that Kennedy had signed the photograph in his presence until I confronted him with a group of other examples of the identical robot pattern. He then admitted that he had gone to the White House to get a signed photograph of the President but had waited outside the office while Kennedy's secretary took the photograph in to the President for his signature.

The reactions of collectors to the news that their treasured autographs are nothing more than robot scrawls can be explosive. Last year a youthful admirer of the Kennedys walked into my office with two photographs, signed by John F. Kennedy and Robert F. Kennedy. When I told him they were not authentic, he asked: "Are you sure?"

I was sure.

With a dramatic flourish, my visitor ripped the photographs into pieces and hurled the fragments into my waste basket.

The abundance of robot signatures is not as bad as it may seem for the young collector. You will find that it adds piquancy and excitement to the chase. To get an *authentic* autograph of President Nixon or Neil Armstrong you will have to outmaneuver or outwit your quarry. One of the best ways is to write to him at his vacation or home address, where he may have the leisure to reply personally. Another good method is to catch him at a speech or rally. Bring along a Bible. For some reason, no public figure has ever refused to put his signature in a Bible, and they make valuable and interesting souvenirs.

Certainly, if you try hard enough and long enough, you will sooner or later get the coveted autograph.

Authentic signature of Richard M. Nixon. Notice how he drops the "ar" from "Richard" and the "on" from "Nixon."

8.

TRAPS FOR THE UNWARY

I SAT IN A dimly lit room of the University Club and examined the document which my host, Professor David Randall, had set before me. Here was the final, unsuccessful exchange of messages between the British and German diplomats, written on the very day World War I broke out! I studied the variously colored inks and the embossed insignia of the British embassy at the top of the first page. "Undoubtedly authentic!" I exclaimed. "Congratulations on discovering a great historic document."

Two days later I had a visit from another dealer, who had just examined the same document in the sunlight and had seen at once that it was actually a facsimile. It had all the telltale signs of lithography, a process of printing on stone which can almost exactly duplicate original writing: the ink in the handwriting and signatures revealed tiny air bubbles, found in facsimiles but never in hand-scrawled ink; all the obvious marks of a handwritten document were missing. (There was no crossing over of strokes in letters, such as the crossbars on the *t*s. If you look at a handwritten *t* under a magnifier, you will see that the crossbar has ploughed through the earlier upright stroke.)

It was an embarrassing experience for me and could have been costly for my friend, but I was reminded again of the great care with which all signatures should be examined. It may be very romantic to peruse a fascinating old paper in pleasing company by the light of a dim yellow lamp, but that's no way to authenticate a rare document.

Stamped signature of Andrew Johnson

There are many traps into which you might fall, and they are the same ones that occasionally catch even experienced dealers. Lithographs are just one example. Our modern presidents, especially Hoover, Truman and Eisenhower, frequently sent out notes signed by lithography that have fooled lots of unwary collectors. Letters of thanks, Christmas greetings, and appeals for funds signed by noted persons usually bear facsimile signatures. Hitler's New Year's cards, printed on his gold-embossed stationery, were almost invariably signed with superb and very deceptive lithographed signatures.

Authentic signature of Franklin D. Roosevelt, 1932 (top). Secretarial signature, 1932 (bottom). The bottom example, one of the most skilled imitations of Roosevelt's signature, was signed only to letters written during his 1932 Presidential campaign.

Steel- or rubber-stamped signatures have also at times proved the undoing of otherwise knowledgeable collectors. Henry VIII and William Penn were both partial to stamps for signing their names. Andrew Johnson was the first American president to use a stamped signature, found on most vellum commissions which bear his name. Theodore Roosevelt, Woodrow Wilson and Franklin D. Roosevelt also had recourse to this method of signing. Stamped signatures may be identified by the same means as lithographed signatures.

You need only examine a suspected autograph carefully to find out whether you have a facsimile or an original. But . . . even if you have an original, it may not be in the handwriting of the alleged signer. In these days of heavy correspondence very few executives sign their own mail. I used to have three secretaries who could and did sign my letters for me. One of them even signed my name to checks which were accepted by my bank.

Imagine, then, the problem which confronts government officials in signing the huge outgoing mail that crosses their desks every day. Most of them delegate the task to one or more secretaries. Franklin D. Roosevelt employed seven different secretaries to sign his mail and Missy LeHand, who was his private secretary for many years, even signed checks for him. During his political career, John F. Kennedy had no less than eighteen different secretaries who put his signature to letters—often very important political letters. Most of President Nixon's White House letters are signed for him by a secretary. When he does sign personally, it is with a rapidly scrawled "R.N." Recently the noted dealer, Paul C. Richards, discovered that President Hoover's secretary had imitated Hoover's signature almost perfectly. Even Eisenhower, who liked to sign all autograph requests personally, finally had to employ a secretary to do the job during the few years before his death. You can spot these signatures by their lack of the middle initial which occurs in all genuine Eisenhower signatures.

Initialed signature of Richard Nixon as President

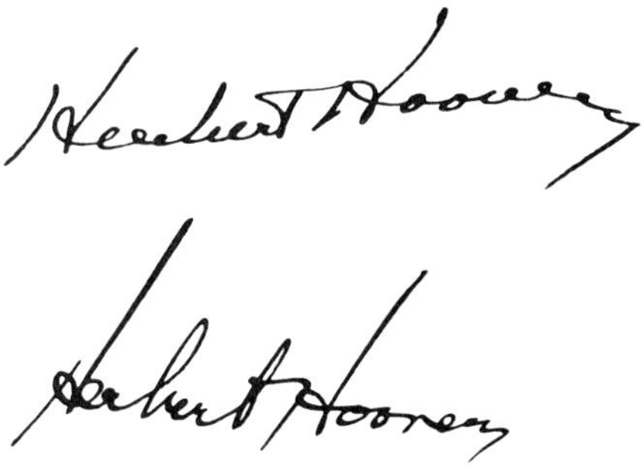

Authentic signature of Herbert Hoover (top). Signature signed for Hoover by his secretary A. G. Shankey (bottom).

Proxy signature of Dwight D. Eisenhower

Perhaps the most common form of presidential proxy signatures are those found on land grants dated after 1833. Andrew Jackson was the first American president to allow a secretary to imitate his signature, but the practice of using a proxy certainly didn't originate with our presidents.

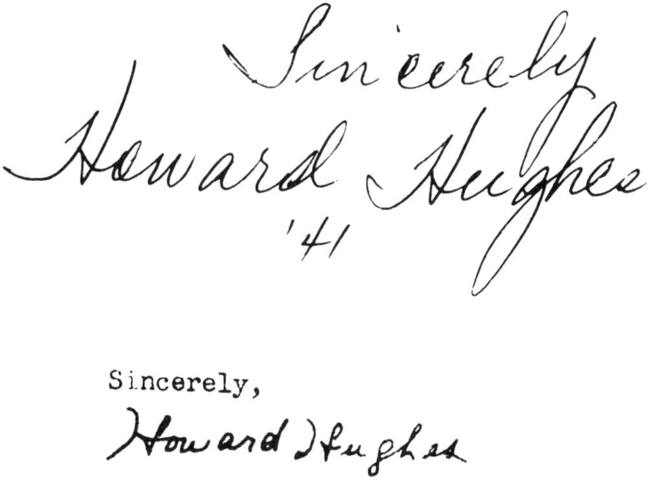

Authentic signature of Howard Hughes, the elusive financier (top). Secretarial signature of Hughes (bottom).

The French kings, especially the Louises, were the first notables to use handwriting secretaries—*secrétaires de main*—to sign routine letters and documents for them. Later, Napoleon permitted an aide to affix his signature, "Bonaparte," to thousands of military appointments, personally signing only those for generals.

Today, every film studio in Hollywood employs several people just to sign autographs, photos and replies

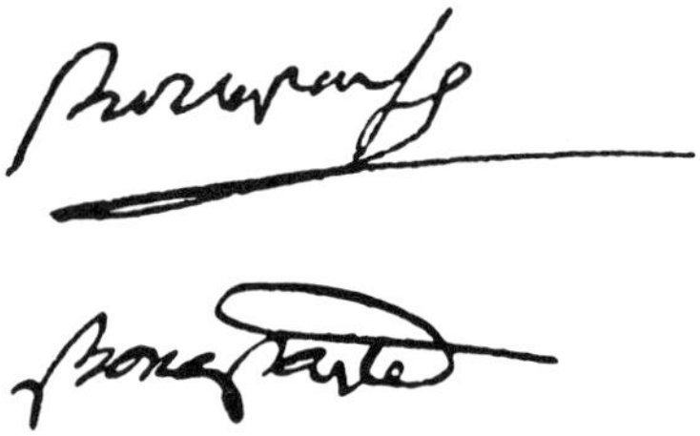

Authentic signature of Napoleon Bonaparte (top). Secretarial signature of Napoleon (bottom). Notice that the secretary omits the flourish under the signature.

to fan mail. One such noted legal forger, Saul Louis Wollman, has been kept busy in his career signing photographs, baseballs, bats, tennis rackets, first editions, courtesy cards, scrolls and records. "My clients," he says, "have included Bing Crosby, Bob Hope, Dinah Shore, Arthur Godfrey, Perry Como, Jack Paar, Mike Wallace, Lucille Ball and dozens of others. When I worked for Mary Pickford, she wasn't able to tell my imitation from her own signature."

As you can see, the alert young collector must be on the lookout for all sorts of autographs that aren't authentic, such as lithographed, stamped, secretarial and even machine signatures. But he will also find that they are merely a few more of the pitfalls and hurdles which help to make the chase more exciting.

9.

THE PRESIDENTS: EVERYBODY'S FAVORITES

"I REMEMBER the first autograph I ever sent away for," recalls Herman Darvick. "It was in February of 1962, and I had just celebrated my sixteenth birthday by spending most of my birthday money for postage. I had decided to begin collecting autographs as a hobby, and I wanted to start by writing to the living Presidents and First Ladies.

"I sent requests for autographs to President and Mrs. Kennedy, Vice-President and Mrs. Johnson, former Presidents Herbert Hoover, Harry S Truman and Dwight D. Eisenhower. I also wrote to former Vice-Presidents John Nance Garner, Henry Wallace and Richard Nixon.

"I was thrilled when I got replies from them all, including the autographs of Mrs. Truman and Mrs. Eisenhower. My collection was on its way!"

When you begin your collection, you, too, may decide to start it with autographs of the President and

Authentic signature of Harry S Truman signed in 1953. Notice how firm and strong the script is!

Authentic signature of Harry S Truman signed in 1966. As a result of a muscular affliction, the signature is very tremulous.

Secretarial signature of Harry S Truman signed in 1971. There is actually very little similarity between this inept imitation and Truman's own signature. Further, the secretary even placed a period after Truman's middle initial "S," and Truman stated on many occasions that the "S" was not an abbreviation and shouldn't have any period after it.

the Vice-President. But you should remember that they are very busy men and it won't be easy to get a genuine signature—much less a letter—from either of them. You may have to be content with a secretarial or robot example, unless you can come up with a shrewdly worded request or are very lucky.

"The worst disappointments I had as a young collector," says David Battan, now a well-known dealer, "were the many rejection letters I got from former President Truman's secretary for letters or signatures. I admired Mr. Truman a great deal and wanted to add a letter from him to my collection. I was very persistent, however, and, as the years passed, Mr. Truman became very generous with his autograph. In fact, he greatly endeared himself to autograph collectors by sending his signature to all who asked for it."

In his later years, Truman rarely signed autographs for collectors. Peter Kanze, a collector, recalls the days when Truman gave his personal attention to signature hunters:

"The first 'good item' that I ever received in the mail was during the late spring of 1964, when I wrote to Truman and asked for his autograph. On June 11, 1964, he replied, 'Dear Peter: The autograph you requested is the signature to this letter. I am glad to send it to you and appreciate your wanting it. Sincerely yours, HARRY S TRUMAN.' I didn't exactly rip open the envelope, but I did spend the whole afternoon calling my friends and bragging about it."

Because they are so often approached by collectors, presidents and ex-presidents are usually quite wary. Herbert Hoover explained it this way: "An autograph collector once asked me for three autographs. I inquired why. He said, 'It takes two of yours to get one of Babe Ruth's.' "

Strangely enough, despite the fact that Babe Ruth was a kind and generous man and often spent an hour or more after every game signing baseballs or autographs for his young fans, his autograph is still, even today, worth twice as much as Hoover's!

If you decide to collect presidential autographs, it's a good idea to think ahead by corralling now the autographs of important statesmen who might some day become president. Those who got Nixon's autograph while he was in Congress or the Senate have a real treasure. If they waited until he was vice-president to go after him, they were generally rewarded only with an Autopen or secretarial signature. As president, he signs virtually nothing for collectors. Even high-ranking political figures receive letters and photographs signed by a secretary or Autopen.

Sooner or later, you'll want to begin collecting autographs of presidents who are no longer living. These autographs, of course, you'll have to get either by trading or, more likely, by buying from dealers or at auction.

The two most sought-after autographs of presidents are those of Washington and Lincoln, and these are apt to cost nearly as much as the rest of the presidents put together. Other desirable and also expensive autographs—rarer than most—are those of John Adams, Thomas Jefferson, James Madison, James K. Polk, Zachary Taylor and John F. Kennedy. Least costly are those of the "forgotten" presidents—John Tyler, Franklin Pierce, James Buchanan and others of like

Signature of Babe Ruth

Signature of Dwight D. Eisenhower

Signature of George Washington

Signature of Abraham Lincoln

Signatures of Franklin Pierce and John Tyler

stature. You can buy their signatures for around $15 to $20 from autograph dealers.

Some older, wealthy collectors deliberately make their collections more challenging and difficult to complete by gathering only letters or documents written while the president was in the White House. This type of collection has one stumbling block—the signature of William Henry Harrison. Harrison died after exactly one month in office, leaving behind a lamentably small supply of presidential autographs. Those which have appeared on the market have brought extremely high prices.

Signature of William Henry Harrison

Most young collectors start their presidential collections with signatures only, and this makes the series easier and much less costly to complete. From the administration of U. S. Grant to the present one, most of the presidents have selectively distributed signed Executive Mansion or White House cards, or signed views of the White House. A collection of such cards is very attractive, although it is quite expensive. Only two Executive Mansion cards by Grant are known, and those authentically signed by Kennedy, Lyndon B. Johnson and Richard Nixon are extremely rare.

The most spectacular and colorful of Presidential documents are commissions and ship's papers. The commissions—appointments of officers or officials—are often engraved on vellum with designs of cannons and swords. They are flamboyant display pieces for any collection. Only slightly less ornamental, the ship's papers were required by law to be issued to every vessel, no matter how small or what its destination, leaving an American port. Many of them were engraved on vellum with a view of a lighthouse or a vessel at the top. Others were printed on paper in three or four languages. Until the time of Lincoln, nearly all ship's papers were personally signed by the president and his secretary of state. Most eagerly sought are those that bear the signatures of both Washington and Jefferson.

If you do decide to specialize in presidential autographs, one thing is certain: You will have many companions and many competitors!

White House card signed by Warren G. Harding

Executive Mansion card signed by Grover Cleveland

1794, Brigadier General

1796, Commander, Army of Italy

1798, Commander, Army of Egypt

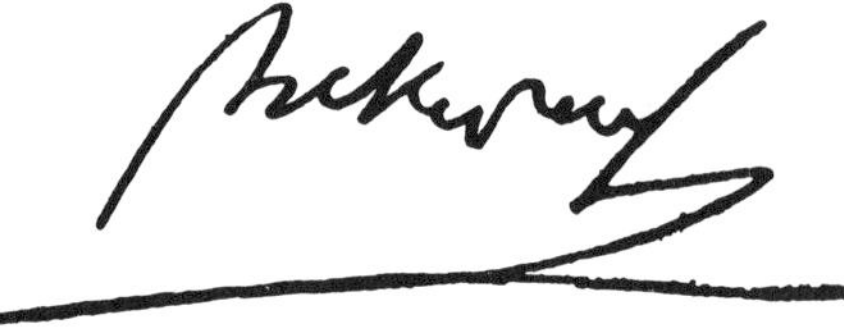

1803, First Consul

1806, Emperor

1808, Emperor

1810, Emperor

1813, Emperor

1815, after Elba

Variant signatures of Napoleon I

10.

STRANGE STORIES ABOUT SIGNATURES

"If you had to pick the strangest, most illegible signature of all time," a collector once asked me, "whose would it be? Napoleon's?"

"Until a decade ago," I told him, "that would have been my choice. Napoleon's handwriting—particularly his signature—was so uncontrolled and erratic that his father-in-law, the Emperor Francis I of Austria, said of him, 'I always knew that man would come to a bad end. He wrote such a villainous hand.' And Francis was more or less correct, as shown by the fact that many of Napoleon's letters have never been fully deciphered!

"But an even stranger signature," I told him, "is one that's much more modern. It is the most illegible signature that I have ever seen of a famous man. It is also the wildest and most impulsive, the most unrestrained. It is the signature of President John F. Kennedy.

As *author of Why England Slept*
(August, 1940)

As ex-Commander of P.T. 109
(October, 1943)

As Congressman (1952)

As President (1962)

As Senator (1960)

Signature signed at a banquet, 1960

(September, 1962)

(May, 1963)

(December, 1960)

Variant signatures of John F. Kennedy

"Kennedy's sputtering, rapid-fire scrawl is almost impossible to read. And since Kennedy never signed his name the same way twice, it takes an expert to recognize a letter or signature of Kennedy."

"Then how," my friend asked me, "can *you* tell if a signature of Kennedy is the real thing, right from his own pen, and not that of a secretary or a robot?"

"That's easy," I told him. "If it's genuine, it won't look like any other signature of Kennedy."

The earliest known signatures of famous men seem very bizarre to us today, because they look more like designs than signatures. The popes of the Middle Ages used a rota signature, a circle with the name incorporated inside. And most of the early emperors and kings stamped their names with a signum ring which had their initials or name worked into a design. Such signatures—and the seals with which they were made—are today very rare and valuable and are eagerly sought by collectors.

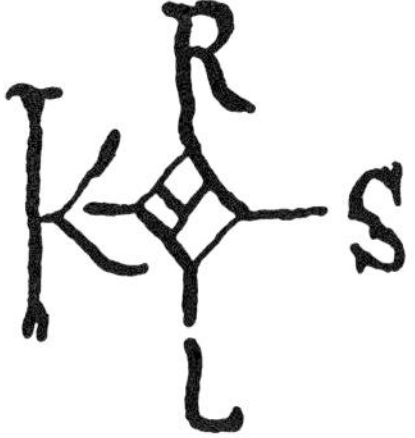

Charlemagne (signum)

Perhaps the most fascinating of all signatures are those of the early American Indians who, because they did not know how to read or write, signed their names with totems, or drawings of animals representing the clan to which they belonged and from which they usually took their names. A member of the bear clan, for example, would usually have a bear in his name. He might be called Running Bear, or Little Bear, or Bear-with-sharp-claws, and he would draw his signature in some form of a bear.

Chief Iron Tail, one of several Indians who posed for the buffalo nickel, signed with his thumb print. Another celebrated Indian, Chief Two Guns White Calf, used a pictograph when signing, as did the

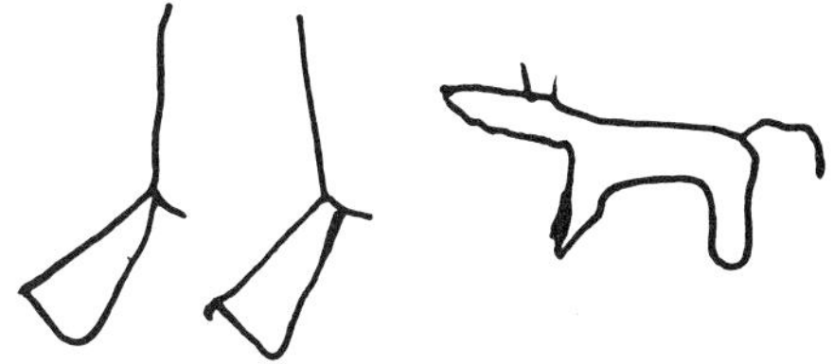

Signature of Chief Two Guns White Calf

Signature of Sitting Bull

Pictographic signature of Sitting Bull

Signature of Geronimo

famous Sioux leader, Sitting Bull. Later in life, Sitting Bull learned to write his name in the white man's way, but he never understood the meaning or sounds of the individual letters in his signature.

The Apache chief, Geronimo, learned to print his name in a most colorful, unusual way. An old lady, who as a young girl had met the chief and had got his autograph, told me: "He printed his signature down the page, as if it were Chinese, writing every letter sideways as he went."

But let's consider the Declaration of Independence. Have you ever looked at a facsimile of it, with the fifty-six signatures of the members of the Continental Congress affixed? Here—on one document—you can study the signatures of some of the most famous and influential men of the eighteenth century.

If you have examined the Declaration, likely the one thing that stands out most in your mind is the huge size of John Hancock's signature, which dominates all fifty-five others. It is reported that after he signed, Hancock said, "King George won't have to put on his spectacles to read my signature!" Hancock's bold scrawl on the Declaration has made his name a synonym for the word "signature."

Signature of John Hancock

Signature of Button Gwinnett

Signature of Reverdy Johnson

One of the smaller signatures on the Declaration of Independence is that of Button Gwinnett, an obscure signer from Georgia. But so rare is his signature—Gwinnett was killed in a duel not long after signing the Declaration—that a letter signed by him once sold at auction for $51,000.

Among nineteenth-century Americans, two stand out as masters of unreadable script. The first is Senator Reverdy Johnson, the famous Civil War states-

Signature of William B. Camp (Comptroller of the Currency). This incredible flourish has been described as resembling a fishing line after a bad cast.

man and minister to England. A Michigan autograph dealer, the late Forest H. Sweet, once offered a batch of Johnson's letters free to anyone who could read them!

Just as erratic a scribbler was the noted newspaper editor, Horace Greeley. There are many stories about his handwriting, the most amusing of which is that, in a moment of anger, he wrote an irate note discharging an employee for incompetence. So illegible was his scrawl that the man later used the note as a letter of recommendation for another job—and he was hired!

Signature of Horace Greeley

Many of the strange and unusual autographs I've told you about are quite costly today, and sometimes difficult to obtain. While you may never own a rare autograph worth a fortune, if you are alert and enterprising you will be able to assemble many unusual and fascinating signatures. If you decide to collect strange signatures, there are several modern ones which you can, with a little good fortune, add to your collection. Noel Coward, the composer and dramatist, has a signature like a hastily constructed fence. And Astronaut Neil Armstrong's signature is very similar and just as fascinating.

Signature of Noel Coward

I asked Herman Darvick to tell me about the strangest autographs in his collection. He wrote to me as follows:

"The really unique autographs in my collection are the signatures of Chernoushka and Zvezdochka. Russian ballet dancers or a Polish wrestling team? No! Roughly translated from the Russian, their names mean Blackie and Little Star, two Russian space dogs, commonly called muttniks.

"As an eager young collector, I addressed a letter to

Dear Mr Darrick!

I send to you the paws-prints of the dogs „Chernoushka" and „Zvezdochka".
Excuse me for a long delay

Very sincerely yours V. Parin

8.1.1966

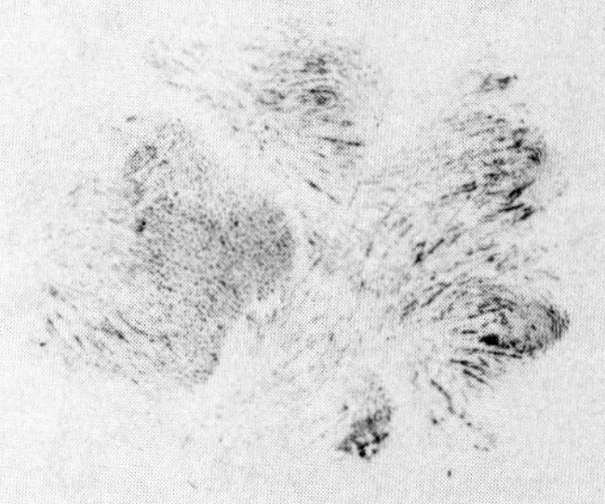

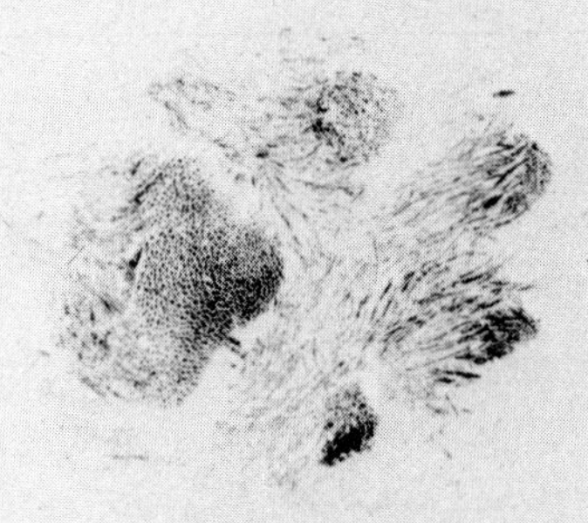

Paw prints of Russian space dogs

'Chernoushka and Zvezdochka, Russian Space Center, Moscow, U.S.S.R.' I began my letter 'Dear Space-dogs' and asked for their paw prints. These two dogs had been launched into orbit in March 1961, in two separate sputniks, the last two tests before Yuri Gagarin became the first man in space on April 12, 1961.

"Eight months later, I received a large envelope in the mail with a dozen colorful Russian stamps postmarked from Moscow. My name and address had been written both in English and in Russian. When I opened the envelope, I tried to remember to whom I had sent an autograph request in Russia. I couldn't remember. Then I looked at the sheet inside on which was a six-line handwritten letter and five ink spots. The letter explained:

" 'Dear Mr. Darvick! I send to you the paws prints of the dogs Chernoushka and Zvezdochka. Excuse me for a long delay. Very sincerely yours, V. Parin, 8-1-1966.' "

Not long ago, I appeared on a television show with the trainer of the dog who is currently playing Lassie in the famous television series. When I told him that my daughter, Carolyn, enjoyed watching the Lassie show, he offered me a photograph of Lassie, signed with her paw print. Since Lassie naturally gets hundreds of letters weekly requesting her photograph, her studio has these photographs mass-produced, with a facsimile paw print. And because Lassie, of course, has none of the historical importance of the Russian space dogs, even an original photograph and paw print would never have anywhere near the value of those of the space dogs. But my daughter will have a lot of fun with it and it will be an interesting addition to any future collection she may form.

I have given you just a few examples of the endless variety of fascinating, strange, sometimes almost frightening examples of famous signatures you can collect. Fortunately, I don't believe it's possible to predict the future by analysing a person's signature. If I did, I'd be afraid to look at some of the signatures of today's famous and important men. As somebody once commented, "Had Belshazzar seen Horace Greeley's handwriting on the wall, he would have been a great deal more frightened than he was!"

11.

ADVENTURES OF BEGINNERS

The first autograph I ever owned cost me a week's pay but it changed the course of my life. I had read in a newspaper that Rudyard Kipling, then my favorite author, received five dollars a word for his stories; but I thought perhaps if I sent him the weekly ten cents I earned for hauling out our furnace ashes, he would be pleased enough with the dime to give me his signature.

I wrote to him, explaining that I was enclosing a week's wages in my letter. Nearly two suspenseful months passed, then came a small envelope with a British three-pence stamp addressed to Charles Hamilton, Esq. I recall vividly how I cherished and fondled and examined Kipling's signature. I was a very ordinary boy in a very ordinary midwestern city and the world's greatest author had taken the time and trouble to write his name for me.

In quick succession I added several other autographs to my collection: Thomas A. Edison and William Howard Taft. I was now launched in the exciting hobby of autograph collecting.

Just recently I chatted with some of the most distinguished collectors in America to find out how they got started.

While relaxing on the Saint Lawrence river, far from the tensions of Washington, Congressman Seymour Halpern of Queens, New York, told me the story of how he began his famous collection of autographs.

"I had just read the autobiography of Edward W. Bok, the famous editor of *The Ladies Home Journal*, in which he relates his adventures as a collector, and it fired my imagination. Why couldn't I, too, write to celebrities and get replies from them? Although I was only thirteen years old, I wrote to President Coolidge and ex-President Taft and received signatures from both. But I wanted something more meaningful, so I began to ask, in my letters to celebrities, 'To what do you attribute your success?'

"I received dozens of fascinating replies. The novelist Thomas Wolfe and the poet John Masefield both answered. I had a little artistic talent, so I sent caricatures to famous people, small sketches I had made, asking them to sign. Most of them did, including the elusive George Bernard Shaw. Adolf Hitler refused; but his secretary, Rudolf Hess, wrote me that Hitler thought my sketch was awful and was sending in its place a signed photograph!"

I asked the Congressman: "Did your autograph collecting help in your political career?"

"Indeed it did!" he told me. "When I was sixteen, as a result of the publicity I had received from my autograph collection, I began to do Sunday features for the Long Island Press. This led to interviews with local political leaders, including Mayor LaGuardia, who took a fancy to me. I campaigned for him, and in 1937 he named me as one of his aides.

"Through the connections I made with politicians while seeking their autographs, I became assistant to Newbold Morris, President of the City Council; and I helped to form the New York State Young Republicans Club, as a result of which I was elected, at 26, to a State Senate seat."

The vice-president of Charles Hamilton Galleries, H. Keith Thompson, Jr., is also interested in politics and once ran for Congress. I asked him to tell me how he became a collector.

"Postage stamps were my first interest," Mr. Thompson told me. "I began to collect them when I was ten years old. I found myself fascinated by the persons, places and events depicted on the stamps. I began writing to heads of state and other notables, asking them to autograph miniature sheets or stamps bearing their portraits. My first successful subject was King Carol II of Rumania, with whom I began a personal correspondence resulting in a twenty-year friendship.

"Franklin D. Roosevelt was also very friendly and helpful to me when I was a beginning collector. As governor, and later as president, he wrote to me about his collecting interests. Even Adolf Hitler, Benito Mussolini, Chaim Weizman and Leon Trotsky autographed philatelic items for me.

"As I grew older, my stamp interests took second place to the general collecting of autographs. I bought primarily from dealers, as far as my limited funds permitted. I didn't specialize exclusively in any one field, but I ordered letters, documents and signed photos which interested and appealed to me."

Rather luckless in his first collecting endeavor was Peter Kanze. "I had long looked forward to the delights of assembling a full set of autographs," Mr. Kanze said, "and as I was especially interested in New York State senators, I aimed for a complete set." Ultimately, he told me, he managed to acquire every one except Joseph Zaretzki. "After six letters to him, I realized that even though I had all of these really beautiful letters of senators, I could never have a complete set and I threw the album aside in exasperation."

David Battan is a successful Fresno, California, autograph dealer, but he, too, began collecting autographs when he was just a boy. "When I was fourteen years old, in junior high school, I was asked, as a special project, to make myself an expert in some field of government. I decided to study the United Nations, and I wrote to the U.S. Ambassador to the United Nations asking him for information to help me in my research.

"Several days later I received a letter personally signed by the ambassador, Warren Austin. I was extremely impressed by the fact that such a busy man would take the time to send a personal letter to a young student. As a result of that letter, I began writing to famous political figures and to build a collection of autographs.

"When I first started collecting, I thought my hobby was unique. But after a few trips to the library, I discovered that there were quite a few dealers in autographs and I was able to find several books on the subject."

Herman Darvick, who also began as a collector, learned an important lesson soon after he began sending requests for autographs.

"I had sent an autograph request to John Steinbeck, who was living in Sag Harbor, New York, at the time. I usually enclosed return postage with my requests; but this time, for some reason, I had forgotten. When I received an answer, it was in an envelope addressed to me in black ink, postmarked 'Sag Harbor, N.Y.' but without a stamp! Inside was a card with five lines written in red ink: 'It is customary on mailing a request of a stranger to enclose an envelope addressed and stamped.'

"On the opposite side of Steinbeck's envelope he had drawn two black lines through the return address, but I managed to read it. I immediately sent off another request to Steinbeck, enclosing a self-addressed, stamped envelope and apologizing for not having done so before. A few days later, I received his autograph on a small card.

"Later I found out that both autographs were genuine and, interestingly enough, the five-line unsigned message of advice is more valuable than the signature. I never again forgot to enclose a self-addressed envelope along with my autograph requests. That's sound advice for all autograph collectors. But don't take chances and expect to get a handwritten note like I did if you don't enclose postage. I was just lucky in this instance. In the vast majority of cases, you won't even get a reply!"

Paul C. Richards began collecting autographs shortly before he started college. "My sophomore year saw my collection growing by leaps and bounds," recalls Mr. Richards. "Robert Frost came to Boston University to give one of his poetry readings. I purchased a paperback edition of his poems and, following his presentation, went backstage where I met the poet for the first time. Mr. Frost signed his autograph for me on the flyleaf of the book. This was the beginning of a friendship with Mr. Frost that lasted until his death. During this period, I purchased as many first editions of Frost's poems as I could locate, and periodically I would visit him at his home in Cambridge, where he would sign and inscribe the books for me. I would inform Mr. Frost of the prices his books and manuscripts were fetching at public auction, and he would be amazed at the value placed on his writings.

"During the four years of our acquaintance, Frost inscribed almost sixty books to me, as well as numerous photographs, his personally imprinted Christmas cards (each containing a poem) and other pieces of ephemera.

"I have continued to add to this collection by purchasing Frost's letters, books and manuscripts at auction and from other dealers. My Frost collection now is one of the largest and finest still in private hands."

While I shouldn't want to hazard a guess at the value of Paul Richards' Robert Frost collection today, the autographs he obtained personally from Frost cost him nothing and doubtless are now worth thousands of dollars!

12.

COLLECTING FOR INVESTMENT

NOT LONG AGO I received a letter from a man whose fifteen-year-old son had just started a collection of autographs. "I am afraid that he is wasting his time and money," he wrote. "But my son tells me that autographs do have value; and to confirm this he has asked me to write to you. I am attaching a list of the autographs in his collection for your comments."

Most of the autographs—mainly signed photographs—had only a modest value, perhaps ten times the cost of postage and stationery to his son. But one signed photo caught my eye. It was of Fidel Castro, the Cuban dictator, who rarely replies to requests for his autographs and almost never signs photos. I had only a few months earlier sold at auction a signed photo of Castro for $425.

I wrote to the boy's father: "Recently I sold a signed photo of Castro for $425, and I must congratulate your son on the high value of his collection. Only a remarkably persuasive letter can beguile the notorious dictator into signing his name. If your son ever decides to sell his collection, I hope he will get in touch with me."

The plight of this youthful collector is one that many young autograph seekers share. He was certain his collection had value, but he had to convince his father. I asked Herman Darvick whether he had ever run into this problem. Mr. Darvick told me that he had:

"I had been collecting autographs for about a year, but my mother thought I was just wasting a lot of money on postage and that I ought to save the money instead.

"I had in my collection four 'Project Mercury' first-day covers, one signed by astronauts Shepard and Grissom, another signed by astronaut Glenn, a third by astronauts Carpenter and Schirra, and a fourth by Cooper and Slayton—the original seven Mercury astronauts. To prove my point, I bought four 'Project Mercury' first-day covers from a stamp dealer at ten cents each. I wrote a letter to the astronauts at NASA in Houston, Texas (eight cents postage) and asked them—there were only seven at that time—to sign the four covers in the same fashion as they had done for me previously. Two weeks later, I received the four covers, all signed the way I'd requested.

"I then wrote a letter to you, Mr. Hamilton, enclosing the four covers (eight more cents postage) offering them for sale. A week later I received your check for $17.50. In less than a month, my initial investment of fifty-six cents had brought me $17.50.

"My mother never again brought up the subject of my wasting my money collecting autographs."

There are many autographs obtainable today which almost certainly will become more valuable in the future. At a recent auction, for example, I offered for sale a signed typescript of excerpts from Douglas MacArthur's speech upon receiving the Sylvanus Thayer Award at West Point on May 12, 1962. A collector had typed out the excerpts and sent the pages to MacArthur for his signature. This fragment of Americana fetched $400!

As I pointed out earlier, the autographs that increase fastest in value are those of intrinsic interest and genuine merit. Mere signatures are not apt to become more valuable, although there are a few exceptions,

There is no substitute for victory.

Let others debate the political issues. You stand as the nation's lifeguard in the swirling seas of discord, its gladiators in the arena of international conflict. Let the civilians argue the merits and demerits of the processes of government....a government sapped by Federal patronage grown too mighty, a nation whose morals have become too low and its taxes too high.

But that is not for your participation. You are the guideposts, the beacons of Duty, Honor, Country.

Band together, for the moment the war tocsin sounds, the Long Gray Line must never fail. If you should fail, a million American dead would rise from their white crosses and thunder Duty, Honor, Country.

The shadows are long for me. The twilight is here. The days of old have gone glimmering, watered by tears, smiled upon by destiny.

I seem to hear the faint call of a bugle, the sound of a far-off drum.

In my dreams I hear again the crash of guns, the strange mutter and rumble of the battlefield.

And in the evening of my memory, always I come back to West Point, and always find there echoes. This is my final roll call with you. And when I cross the road, my last thought will be "The Corps, The Corps, The Corps."

I bid you farewell.

Excerpts from speech given by General of the Army Douglas MacArthur upon his receiving the Sylvanus Thayer Award at West Point on May 12, 1962

Excerpts from a speech, signed by Douglas MacArthur

like those of Washington and Lincoln. Of more interest are signed photographs and first-day covers.

But I urge all youthful collectors to seek out interesting letters and signed statements or proclamations from famous men and women. Think how much more exciting would be a comment signed by Neil Armstrong describing his emotions on first setting foot on the moon than a mere pictorial first-day cover.

If you want to collect autographs that will be almost certain to increase in value, avoid the ordinary and the obvious! Get your heroes to write to you about their exploits—in literature, in history, in music, in science. Ask James Jones—or any author you especially like—who of all his characters is his favorite. Or ask Vice-President Agnew if he would recommend a career in politics for a young man or woman. Or you could ask him if he would rather be president than vice-president.

There are a thousand celebrated people waiting for your letters, provided you write interesting and provocative letters; and if you use the methods I have suggested, you will find yourself one day with a valuable and important collection.

It's also great fun to try and anticipate who will be the next president or governor. If you decide to write to the candidates, be sure to ask an interesting question. Most famous men and women are usually too burdened with problems to send their signatures to a boy or girl. But they will often take the time to answer a sincere letter, asking a question like, "What was your favorite subject when you were in school?"

If you can afford to buy from dealers or at auction, my advice about the autographs most likely to increase in value is this: collect presidents, or other American autographs. Avoid foreign material, which has never kept pace pricewise with American autographs. Many presidential documents are today selling for twenty or more times as much as ten years ago.

If you are successful and happy in collecting for profit, you may someday want to try to become a dealer, as many collectors before you have

[PUBLIC LAW 328—77TH CONGRESS]

[CHAPTER 561—1ST SESSION]

[S. J. Res. 116]

JOINT RESOLUTION

Declaring that a state of war exists between the Imperial Government of Japan and the Government and the people of the United States and making provisions to prosecute the same.

Whereas the Imperial Government of Japan has committed unprovoked acts of war against the Government and the people of the United States of America: Therefore be it

Resolved by the Senate and House of Representatives of the United States of America in Congress assembled, That the state of war between the United States and the Imperial Government of Japan which has thus been thrust upon the United States is hereby formally declared; and the President is hereby authorized and directed to employ the entire naval and military forces of the United States and the resources of the Government to carry on war against the Imperial Government of Japan; and, to bring the conflict to a successful termination, all of the resources of the country are hereby pledged by the Congress of the United States.

Approved, December 8, 1941, 4:10 p. m., E. S. T.

Sam Rayburn Harry Truman

H A Wallace

Official printing of the United States declaration of war against Japan, signed for a collector by Harry S Truman, House Speaker Sam Rayburn, and Vice-President Henry A. Wallace

B 106

USHIBORI: A JUNK MOORED AMONG REEDS
One of the *Thirty-six views of FUJI*
Japanese Colour-print by Hokusai (1760-1849)
(Size 10 in. × 14⅝ in.)

British Museum

Hamden Conn May 10

Dear Mrs. Carmichael /

I had 'em. But I've long since destroyed and even forgotten them.

I once had something worse: the refusal of the dedication of The Skin of our Teeth by a dear friend, a much admired and very intelligent Englishwoman who felt that the play was "defeatist."

Sorry I cannot add to your collection of rejection slips. All best wishes to the project. Sincerely

Thornton Wilder

Holograph letter on a postcard of Thornton Wilder, in reply to an interesting query: Had he ever received any rejection slips?

done. As you gain in knowledge and experience, you may want to try and supplement your income or even try becoming a full-time dealer. If so, you will find it a rewarding profession.

The best way to start is to get your mailing list from the Universal Autograph Collectors Club, which is the ideal collector's association for young people, and from the Manuscript Society, which consists mostly of older, wealthier collectors. Then, with intelligence and knowledge and with the energy and desire it takes to succeed in any profession, you will begin to achieve success.

The more you learn about history, literature, music and science, the more successful you will be, whether as a collector or a dealer. And, of course, you will have to familiarize yourself with the basic facts about papers, inks, watermarks and handwriting styles.

One thing is certain. There seems to be no end to the upward spiral in the value of autographs. Whatever you decide to collect, and however you decide to collect, I am certain that in coming years your collection will prove to be not only a valuable cultural heritage but a splendid investment as well!

APPENDIXES

Compiled by HERMAN M. DARVICK
President, Universal Autograph Collector's Club

AUTOGRAPH DEALERS

Abraham Lincoln Book Shop
18 East Chestnut Street
Chicago, Illinois 60611

Laurence C. Affron, Autographs
711 South Flagler
West Palm Beach, Florida 33401

Conway Barker
1231 Sunset Lane, P.O. Box 35
La Marque, Texas 77568

Robert F. Batchelder
1 West Butler Avenue
Ambler, Pennsylvania 19002

David Battan, Autographs
P.O. Box 2212
Fresno, California 93720

Walter R. Benjamin, Autographs
790 Madison Avenue
New York, New York 10021

Robert K. Black
P.O. Box 856
Upper Montclair, New Jersey 07043

Maury A. Bromson Associates, Inc.
195 Commonwealth Avenue
Boston, Massachusetts 02116

Carnegie Book Shop
140 East 59th Street
New York, New York 10022

Herman M. Darvick, Autographs
3109 Brighton 7th Street
Brooklyn, New York 11235

Bruce Gimelson Autographs, Inc.
Fort Washington Industrial Park
Fort Washington, Pennsylvania 19034

Goodspeed's Book Shop, Inc.
18 Beacon Street
Boston, Massachusetts 02108

Charles Hamilton Galleries, Inc.
25 East 77th Street
New York, New York 10021

Doris Harris, Autographs
6381 Hollywood Blvd.
Los Angeles, California 90028

Paul F. Hoag
4417 Allcott Ave.
Sherman Oaks, California 91403

King V. Hostick
901 College Avenue
Springfield, Illinois 62704

John Howell, Books
434 Post Street
San Francisco, California 94102

Curtis Iddings, Jr.
Box 77
Stuarts Draft, Virginia 24477

Dr. Milton Kronovet
881 C. Balmoral Court
Lakewood, New Jersey 08701

Laurence Lingle, Bookseller
3137 Lubbock Avenue
Fort Worth, Texas 76109

James Lowe, Autographs
219 East 70th Street, Box 97
New York, New York 10021

Lester J. Meadows
4207 Matilija Avenue
Sherman Oaks, California 91403

Howard Mott
Sheffield, Massachusetts 01257

Kenneth Nebenzahl, Inc.
333 North Michigan Avenue
Chicago, Illinois 60601

Julia Sweet Newman
P.O. Box 156
Battle Creek, Michigan 49016

Kenneth W. Rendell, Inc.
62 Bristol Road
Somerville, Massachusetts 02144

Paul C. Richards, Autographs
49 Village Drive
Bridgewater, Massachusetts 02324

Joseph Rubinfine
R.F.D. No. 1
Pleasantville, New Jersey 08232

Charles Sessler
1308 Walnut Street
Philadelphia, Pennsylvania 19107

Rosejeanne Slifer
30 Park Avenue
New York, New York 10016

Western Hemisphere, Inc.
1613 Central Street
Stoughton, Massachusetts 02072

AUTOGRAPH AUCTION HOUSES

Americana Mail Auction
4015 Kilmer Avenue
Allentown, Pennsylvania 18104

Bruce Gimelson Autographs, Inc.
Fort Washington Industrial Park
Fort Washington, Pennsylvania 19034

Charles Hamilton Galleries, Inc.
25 East 77th Street
New York, New York 10021

Parke-Bernet Galleries, Inc.
980 Madison Avenue
New York, New York 10021

Swann Galleries, Inc.
117 East 24th Street
New York, New York 10010

AUTOGRAPH PERIODICALS

Manuscripts ($10 annually, published quarterly)
The Manuscript Society
Secretary, Kenneth W. Duckett
Morris Library
Southern Illinois University
Carbondale, Illinois 62901

The Pen and Quill ($6 annually, published monthly)
Universal Autograph Collector's Club
Editor, Henry G. Mazlen
1211 Avenue I
Brooklyn, New York 11230

The Sports Trader ($5 annually, published monthly)
P.O. Box 909
Cupertino, California 95104

ONE HUNDRED WORLD NOTABLES

The President of the United States
1600 Pennsylvania Avenue
Washington, D.C. 20500

Justices of the Supreme Court of the United States
Supreme Court of the United States
1 First Street, N.E.
Washington, D.C. 20543

United States Ambassador to the United Nations
Waldorf Towers
Waldorf Astoria Hotel
New York, New York 10022

American astronauts
Manned Spacecraft Center
NASA
Houston, Texas 77058

Russian cosmonauts
Academy of Sciences
Leninsky Prospekt 14
Moscow, U.S.S.R.

Henry Aaron, baseball star
Atlanta Braves
Atlanta Stadium
Atlanta, Georgia 30312

Bella S. Abzug, U.S. Congresswoman
Longworth Office Building
Washington, D.C. 20515

Spiro T. Agnew, U.S. Vice President
2600 Connecticut Avenue, N.W.
Washington, D.C. 20008

Carl Albert, U.S. Speaker of the House
4101 Cathedral Avenue, N.W.
Washington, D.C. 20016

Henry Armstrong, boxing champion
4327 Shreve Street
St. Louis, Missouri 63115

Miguel Angel Asturias, Nobel literature prizewinner
73 Rue de Courcelles
Paris 8e, France

Burt Bacharach, composer
166 East 61st Street
New York, New York 10021

Bao-Dai, Vietnamese Emperor
Nice,
Alpes Maritimes, France

David Ben-Gurion, Israeli statesman
Sdeh Boker, Israel

Thomas Hart Benton, American artist
3616 Belleview Avenue
Kansas City, Missouri 64111

Irving Berlin, composer
1290 Avenue of the Americas
New York, New York 10019

Shirley Temple Black
Woodside, California

James J. Braddock, boxing champion
7712 Park Avenue
North Bergen, New Jersey 07047

Omar N. Bradley, General of the Army
630 Fifth Avenue
New York, New York 10020

Warren E. Burger, Chief Justice of the United States
3111 North Rochester Street
Arlington, Virginia 22213

William B. Camp, Comptroller of the Currency
Main Treasury Building
Washington, D.C. 20220

René Cassin, Nobel peace prizewinner
36, Quai de Bethune
Paris 4e, France

Marc Chagall, artist
Vence
Alpes Maritimes, France

Charles Chaplin, actor-comedian
Vevey, Switzerland

Mark W. Clark, U.S. general
Francis Marrin Hotel
Charleston, South Carolina 29402

Van Cliburn, pianist
808 S. Martin
Kilgore, Texas 75662

Terence Cardinal Cooke, Archbishop of New York
451 Madison Avenue
New York, New York 10022

Salvador Dali, artist
Hotel St. Regis
5th Avenue and 55th Street
New York, New York 10022

Karl Dönitz, Nazi führer
2055 Aumühle (Holstein)
Pfingstholzallee 4
West Germany

David Douglas Duncan, photo-journalist
Castellaras 53
Mouans-Sartoux
Alpes Maritimes, France

Jimmy Durante, actor-comedian
511 N. Beverly Drive
Beverly Hills, California 90210

Sir Anthony Eden (Lord Avon), British statesman
Manor House
Alvediston, Salisbury
Wiltshire, England, United Kingdom

Ludwig Erhard,
West German statesman
53 Bonn
Johanniterstrasse 8
Bonn, West Germany

James A. Farley, former U.S.
postmaster general
301 Park Avenue
New York, New York 10022

James Farmer, civil rights leader
165 Park Row
New York, New York 10038

Robert H. Finch, former U.S.
cabinet member
820 Southwick Way
Sacramento, California 95825

Henry Ford II, automobile
manufacturer
Grosse Pointe Farms, Michigan 48236

David Frost, television performer
46 Egerton Crescent
London S.W. 3, England, U. K.

Buckminster Fuller, engineer-architect
407 South Forest Street
Carbondale, Illinois 62901

J. Paul Getty, oil executive
Sutton Place, near Guildford
Surrey, England, U. K.

Billy Graham, evangelist
1300 Harmon Place
Minneapolis, Minnesota 55403

Otto Graham, football star
10800 Pleasant Hill
Potomac, Maryland 20854

Huntington Hartford, financier
420 Lexington Avenue
New York, New York 10017

Helen Hayes, actress
Nyack, New York 10960

Hubert H. Humphrey, U.S.
Vice President
550 N. Street, S.W.
Washington, D.C. 20024

Mrs. Lady Bird Johnson, First Lady
LBJ Ranch
Stonewall, Texas 78671

Janos Kadar, Hungarian leader
Socialist Workers' Party
Budapest, Hungary

Edward M. Kennedy, U.S. Senator
636 Chain Bridge Road
McLean, Virginia 22101

Alf M. Landon, U.S. presidential
candidate
1001 Filmore Street
Topeka, Kansas 66604

John V. Lindsay, Mayor of
New York City
Gracie Mansion, East End Avenue
New York, New York 10028

Walter Lippmann, journalist
3525 Woodley Road, N.W.
Washington, D.C. 20016

Henry Cabot Lodge, U.S. politician
275 Hale Street
Beverly, Massachusetts 01915

Robert Lowell, Jr., poet
15 W. 67th Street
New York, New York

Harold Macmillan, British statesman
Birch Grove House, Chelward Gate
Haywards Heath
Sussex, England, U. K.

Joseph Mankiewicz, film director
129 East 71st Street
New York, New York 10021

Mickey Mantle, baseball star
5730 Watson Circle
Dallas, Texas 75223

Annunzio Paolo Mantovani,
orchestra conductor
Greensleeves, Burton Road
Branksome Park
Dorset, England, U. K.

Thurgood Marshall, Supreme Court
Justice
6233 Lakeview Drive
Falls Church, Virginia 22041

Robert B. Mathias, Congressman,
Olympic star
3235 Valley Lane
Falls Church, Virginia 22044

Willie Mays, baseball star
54 Mendosa Avenue
San Francisco, California 94116

Marshall McLuhan, author
29 Wells Hill Avenue
Toronto 4, Ontario, Canada

Gian-Carlo Menotti, composer
"Capricorn"
Mt. Kisco, New York

Montgomery of Alamein,
Field Marshal
Isington Mill, Alton
Hampshire, England, U. K.

Thomas H. Moorer,
Admiral of the U.S. Navy
(Chairman, Joint Chiefs of Staff)
402 Barbour Street
Eufaula, Alabama 36027

Edmund S. Muskie, U.S. Senator
5409 Albia Road, N.W.
Washington, D.C. 20016

Guizarilal Nanda, Indian statesman
6 Hastings Road
New Delhi, India

Julius K. Nyerere, Tanzanian President
State House
Dar es Salaam, Tanzania

Hermann J. Oberth, rocket pioneer
8501 Feucht
Untere Kellerstrasse 13
German Federal Republic

Laurence, Lord Olivier, actor
4 Royal Crescent
Brighton, Sussex, England

Eugene Ormandy, orchestra conductor
230 South 15th Street
Philadelphia, Pennsylvania 19102

Jesse Owens, Olympic star
4800 Chicago Beach Drive
Chicago, Illinois 60600

Linus C. Pauling, Nobel chemistry
and peace prizewinner
Salmon Creek
Big Sur, California 93920

Philip, Prince Consort of England
Buckingham Palace
London S.W. 1
England

Otto Preminger, film producer
711 Fifth Avenue
New York, New York 10022

Isador Rabi, Nobel physics
prizewinner
450 Riverside Drive
New York, New York 10027

Nelson A. Rockefeller, New York,
governor
Pocantico Hills
North Tarrytown, New York

Norman Rockwell, artist
Stockbridge, Massachusetts 01262

Richard Rodgers, composer
598 Madison Avenue
New York, New York 10022

William P. Rogers, U.S. cabinet
member
7007 Glenbrook Road
Bethesda, Maryland 20014

Carlos P. Romulo, Philippine
statesman
74 McKinley Road
Forbes Park, Makati,
Rizal, the Philippines

Artur Rubinstein, pianist
80, Avenue Foch
Paris, France

Albert B. Sabin, polio vaccine pioneer
7420 E. Aracoma Drive
Cincinnati, Ohio 45237

Jonas E. Salk, polio vaccine pioneer
2444 Ellentown Road
La Jolla, California 92037

Arthur Schlesinger, Jr., author
166 East 61st Street
New York, New York 10021

Charles Schulz, "Peanuts" cartoonist
2162 Coffee Lane
Sebastopol, California 95472

Glenn T. Seaborg, nuclear chemist-physicist
3825 Harrison Street, N.W.
Washington, D.C. 20015

Souvanna Phouma, Laotian prime minister
Domaine du Nongthevada
Vientiane, Laos

Carl Spaatz, U.S. Air Force general
5 Grafton Street
Chevy Chase, Maryland 20015

Edward Teller, nuclear physicist
1573 Hawthorne Terrace
Berkeley, California 94708

Harold C. Urey, Nobel chemistry prizewinner
7890 Torrey Lane
La Jolla, California 92037

Rudy Vallee, orchestra leader, singer
7430 Pyramid Place
Hollywood, California 90028

James Van Allen, physicist
5 Woodland Mounds Road
R.F.D. 5
Iowa City, Iowa 52240

George C. Wallace, Alabama governor
State Capitol
Montgomery, Alabama 36100

Earl Warren, former Chief Justice
Sheraton-Park Hotel
Washington, D.C. 20008

William C. Westmoreland, U.S. Army general
Chief of Staff, U.S. Army
Washington, D.C. 20310

Roy Wilkins, civil rights leader
147-15 Village Road
Jamaica, New York 11635

Tennessee Williams, playwright
c/o Audrey Wood
Ashley-Steiner Famous Artists, Inc.
555 Madison Avenue
New York, New York 10022

Vladimir Zworykin, television pioneer
103 Battle Road Circle
Princeton, New Jersey 08540

RECOMMENDED READING

Benjamin, Mary A. *Autographs: A Key to Collecting*. New York, 1946. An excellent and reliable manual, with detailed discussions of some of the complicated aspects of collecting.

Hamilton, Charles. *Collecting Autographs and Manuscripts*. Second edition. Norman, Okla., 1970. A complete guide to autograph collecting with nearly 1,000 facsimiles.

Hamilton, Charles. *Scribblers and Scoundrels*. New York, 1968. An exciting account of Hamilton's adventures with manuscript thieves and forgers. Copiously illustrated.

Madigan, Thomas F. *Word Shadows of the Great*. New York, 1930. Zestful introduction to autograph collecting by one of America's great dealers.

Scott, Henry T. *Autograph Collecting*. London, 1894. The charter manual on autographs, crammed with details, with many facsimiles.